# Hands-On
# GEOMETRY
Constructions With a Straightedge and Compass

# Hands-On GEOMETRY

## Constructions With a Straightedge and Compass

## Christopher M. Freeman

Routledge
Taylor & Francis Group

NEW YORK AND LONDON

First published in 2010 by Prufrock Press Inc.

Published 2021 by Routledge
605 Third Avenue, New York, NY 10017
2 Park Square, Milton Park, Abingdon, Oxon OX14 4RN

*Routledge is an imprint of the Taylor & Francis Group, an informa business*

Copyright © 2010 by Taylor & Francis Group

Production Design by Marjorie Parker

ISBN 13: 978-1-5936-3418-6 (pbk)

DOI: 10.4324/9781003235477

# Dedication

This book is dedicated to my wife, Maria, with gratitude for her tireless support and confidence, and to our children, all of whom love constructions: to Clara, whose eagerness with the first lessons convinced me of their value; to Edward, who liked constructions so well, he took his compass with him on vacation; and to John, who someday will draw his constructions in the finished book.

# Contents

# Acknowledgements

Thanks to Hanna Goldschmidt, mentor, colleague, and friend, under whose direction I first taught geometry; to Bobbi Nelson, fellow geometry teacher, who eagerly adopted these lessons into her classes, made valuable suggestions, and encouraged me to write more; to Paul Gunty, Shirley Holbrook, and all of my colleagues for their ideas and inspiration; to Joan Franklin Smutny, Director of the Center for Gifted at National-Louis University, for her perennial encouragement; to Gretchen Sparling and Jennifer Robins at Prufrock Press for their excellent suggestions; and to the hundreds of children in the "Worlds of Wisdom and Wonder" programs and at The University of Chicago Laboratory Schools who enjoyed these lessons and helped me improve them.

# Introduction

The lessons in *Hands-On Geometry* were written for gifted students in grades 4–6. Older students also enjoy them, and they provide a kinesthetic supplement for a high school geometry class. Students of all ages enjoy using their own hands to draw precise constructions with the simple compass and straightedge tools that have been used for thousands of years.

I have tested these lessons in my own classes, revising and clarifying the step-by-step directions and sample diagrams so that students can work independently. The lessons may be assigned to a whole group or given to an individual student; students may work on them during class or at home. The completed constructions can be assessed at a glance.

## Materials Needed

I provide a 6-inch clear plastic ruler and a compass for each student to use during class. Make sure the compass pencils are sharp. I recommend that each student purchase a higher quality compass for his or her own use (these usually cost about $10). They should choose a compass that is easy to adjust but will maintain a constant radius while drawing. My own compass has lasted 25 years of frequent use.

## Classroom Management

I make separate photocopies of each lesson and keep them readily at hand so each student can work independently, turn in a finished construction, and pick up the next lesson.

On the first day of instruction, it is important to demonstrate proper technique. I gather students around me and show them how to draw a circle:

- Hold the compass at the top, not by the pencil.
- Use the other hand to press the sharp point against the paper.
- Lean the compass in the direction that you will move it, so that the pencil glides over the ridges in the paper rather than jamming into them.
- Draw light, thin arcs, which are more precise than dark, thick ones.

I also demonstrate how to connect two points with a straight line, which is not at all trivial for many students.

- First, sharpen the pencil!
- Slide the straightedge so that it is precisely adjacent to the two points, and hold it in place with one hand.
- Put the pencil tip in the center of one of the points.

- Tilt the pencil so it rests against the straightedge; adjust the straightedge if necessary.
- Lean the pencil in the direction that you will move it (as if it were a paintbrush), and be sure that the line goes right through the center of both points.

These skills are fundamental, and students are eager to master them.

After the first day, students can work at their own pace, lesson by lesson. As promptly as I can, I check each construction for correct procedure and precision, and I work with individual students to correct any incorrect techniques. I set high standards for precision, sometimes even erasing student work and requiring it to be done again. Students of all ages take great pride in their work well done. I give each lesson a grade of √, +, or ++ (one plus for correct procedure, one for precision). Students strive a little harder to receive two plusses! I ask students to color the petals in their regular octagon construction, Lesson 2.7, and some students enjoy decorating their dodecagon into a clock in Lesson 2.8; I display these on a bulletin board.

## Learning Objectives

In Chapter 1, students practice the technique of using a compass and straightedge, constructing an equilateral triangle, concentric circles, and a regular hexagon.

In Chapter 2, students justify the basic constructions with properties of kites: The main diagonal of a kite is perpendicular to the other diagonal, bisects the other diagonal, and bisects the vertex angle. Hence, to construct a perpendicular, a midpoint, or an angle bisector, we create an appropriate kite. Students use these procedures to construct a square, a regular octagon, and a regular dodecagon.

In Chapter 3, students construct the altitudes, angle bisectors, perpendicular bisectors, and medians of a triangle, which are concurrent at the orthocenter, incenter, circumcenter, and centroid. They also construct the inscribed and circumscribed circles of a triangle, and they construct their centroid on cardboard, cut out the triangle, and balance it on the sharp point of their compass.

In Chapter 4, students use perpendiculars to construct parallel lines, rectangles, and a square, and they formulate conjectures about the properties of rectangles and their diagonals.

In Chapter 5, students use oblique lines to construct a parallelogram; students formulate conjectures about the properties of parallelograms and use these properties to find three different methods of constructing parallelograms.

In Chapter 6, students use three given sides, two angles and the included side, or two sides and the included angle to construct unique triangles; these constructions establish the logical basis for using SSS, ASA, and SAS to prove triangles congruent.

In Chapter 7, students peer into the infinitesimal by connecting the midpoints of a quadrilateral in successive iterations; they also construct a golden rectangle and a regular pentagon.

## NCTM Standards

The activities in *Hands-On Geometry* are aligned with national education standards set by the National Council of Teachers of Mathematics (NCTM).

Geometry Standard 1 expects all students to analyze various geometric shapes, to formulate conjectures about their characteristic properties, and to reason logically to justify these conjectures. Every construction activity in this book fulfills this standard. Constructions provide a *purpose* for geometric inquiry: When a student understands the properties of a figure, he or she can use those properties to construct it correctly.

Geometry Standard 4 expects students to construct geometric figures using a variety of tools. It is to be hoped that every geometry student has the opportunity to use computer software for constructing geometric figures, such as The Geometer's Sketchpad or Cabri. My own geometry students use computers extensively in class. But I have found that students find it even more satisfying to draw their constructions by hand.

The NCTM *Focal Points* emphasize that elementary school students need to develop geometric intuition in math class through drawing and analyzing two-dimensional figures; this is precisely what the lessons in *Hands-On Geometry* accomplish.

## A Final Word

Hundreds of my own students have loved these construction activities. I have written this book in hopes that you and your students will enjoy them too.

# Chapter 1:
# Lines and Arcs

 DOI: 10.4324/9781003235477-1

Name_____    Date_____

# Introduction: The Straightedge and Compass Tools

For more than 2,000 years, mathematicians have used two basic tools to construct geometric figures: a **compass** to draw circles, and a **straightedge** to draw lines. With these simple tools, you will learn to construct triangles, hexagons, squares, kites, perpendicular lines, parallel lines, and lots of other figures.

A compass has a sharp point at one end to hold it steady at the center of the circle, and it has a pencil point at the other end to draw the circle. The distance between the sharp point and the pencil point is called the **radius**. You will use a compass to draw circles and arcs. To draw a straight line, you will pull a pencil tip along a straightedge. A straightedge is different from a ruler, because a straightedge has no marks on it. If you use a ruler, you should ignore the inch or centimeter markings. To measure length, you will use the radius of the compass.

# Lesson 1.1
# Construct a Circle by Center and Point

A point is a location. We often represent a point with a dot (.), but any dot is really too big because the point is at the center of the dot. We name points with capital letters, like points C and P below.

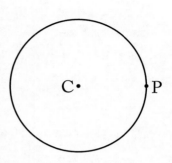

One way to construct a circle starts with one point that will be its center and another point that will be on the circle. Follow the directions below to construct the circle with center C and passing through P. Your construction will look like the picture to the right.

1. Put the sharp point of the compass onto C and hold it there.

2. Adjust the compass radius so that the pencil point rests gently on the point P.

3. Hold the compass at its top, not by the pencil

4. Lean the compass slightly in the direction you want to draw.

5. Start drawing the circle through P; if the curve doesn't go exactly through the center of point P, adjust the radius and start again.

6. Lightly draw the circle with your compass.

•
C

•
P

# Lesson 1.2
# Construct a Line and an Equilateral Triangle

A basic postulate of geometry is that *two points determine a line.* In practice, drawing this line is not as trivial as it may sound. If you work carefully, your construction will look like the picture below. Follow the directions below to construct a line.

1. Place your straightedge *just under* the two points P and Q below. Hold it steady.

2. As you pull your pencil along the straightedge, make sure that the pencil tip goes through the *center* of each point. If not, change the angle of your pencil, or adjust your straightedge. Be precise! Make sure your pencil is sharp.

3. Draw an arrowhead at each end of your line.

The arrowheads indicate that **lines** go on forever in both directions. We name a line using any two points on it with a line symbol above them, such as $\overleftrightarrow{PQ}$ . The piece of a line between two **endpoints** (like P and Q above) is called a **line segment**, or **segment** for short. We name a segment using its two endpoints with a bar on top, such as $\overline{PQ}$ . Segments don't go on forever, they end at their endpoints.

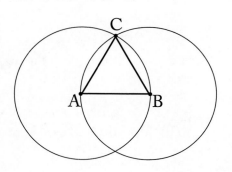

Now you will construct an **equilateral triangle**, in which all three sides are segments of equal length. Your construction will look like the picture to the right.

1. Use your straightedge to construct the line segment $\overline{AB}$.

2. Construct a circle with center A and passing through B.

3. Construct another circle with center B and passing through A.

4. Locate a point where the two circles intersect and label it C. (You don't need to draw a dot because the location where two circles cross *is* a point.)

5. Use your straightedge to construct segments $\overline{AC}$ and $\overline{BC}$. You now have equilateral $\triangle ABC$!

•
A

•
B

# Lesson 1.3
# Draw an Arc and Copy a Segment

Just as a segment is a piece of a line, an **arc** is a piece of a circle.
Which point, A, B, or C, is the **center of the arc** shown below? _____

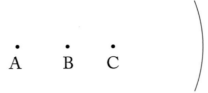

    To check your answer, put the sharp point of your compass on A, adjust your radius, and try to draw the arc. Then put the sharp point on B and try to draw the arc. Then repeat using point C. (Was your answer correct?)

    To **copy a segment** means to make another segment with the same length. Don't use a ruler to measure length—use the radius of your compass! When you follow the directions below, you will construct a copy of segment $\overline{EF}$, called $\overline{PQ}$. Your construction will look like this picture:

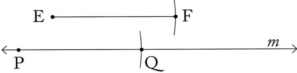

Use segment $\overline{EF}$ and line *m*, below.
1. Anywhere on the line *m*, mark a tiny dot and label it P.

2. Put the sharp point of your compass on E, and adjust the radius so you can draw a short arc through F.

3. Don't change the radius, but move the sharp point to P and draw a short arc that crosses line *m*.

4. Label the point where the arc crosses the line, Q.

5. $\overline{PQ}$ is a copy of $\overline{EF}$, because it has the same length.

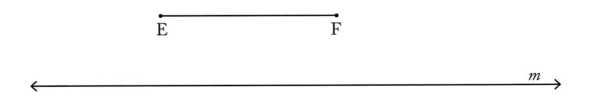

    When we *name* a segment, we put a bar on top, as with $\overline{PQ}$. When we refer to the *length* of a segment, we don't put a bar on top. Thus "PQ" means the length of $\overline{PQ}$, which is the distance from P to Q. Because PQ and EF are numbers, we can write PQ = EF to mean that the segments have the same length.

# Lesson 1.4
# Construct Equally Spaced Concentric Circles

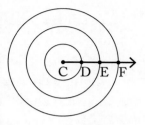

**Concentric circles** have the same center. If they are equally spaced, they will look like a target, as shown to the right. To construct these circles, we don't need the entire line $\overleftrightarrow{CD}$, we just need the part of the line that starts at C and extends to the right through D and beyond. A part of a line that has one endpoint but extends infinitely far in the other direction is called a **ray**. Rays are named with the endpoint first, some other point on the ray second, and a ray symbol on top. The ray we need for the construction of the following concentric circles is named $\overrightarrow{CD}$.

Follow the directions below to construct equally spaced concentric circles.

1. Use your straightedge to construct the ray $\overrightarrow{CD}$, starting at C and passing through D and beyond to the edge of the page.

2. Draw the circle with center C and passing through D.

3. Keeping the radius CD, draw a short arc with center D and crossing the ray on the right side of D. Label the intersection point E.

4. Keeping the same radius, draw a short arc with center E and crossing the ray on the right side of E. Label the intersection point F.

5. Draw the circle with center C and passing through E.

6. Draw the circle with center C and passing through F.

Ċ        Ḋ

# Lesson 1.5
## Construct a Regular Hexagon

A **regular hexagon** has six equal sides and six equal angles. Six equilateral triangles fit together to form a regular hexagon.

Your challenge is to figure out how to construct a regular hexagon, called HEXAGO, when given one side, $\overline{\text{HE}}$. The picture to the right shows just the hexagon and triangles, it does not show the circles or arcs needed to construct it.

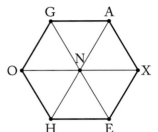

Don't try to draw a hexagon with just a straightedge! You will need to use your compass to draw circles or arcs in order to put the points N, O, G, A, and X in their proper places. As you work, *never erase construction arcs!* Leave your arcs to illustrate your method.

Hint: Use the method shown in Lesson 1.2 to construct equilateral triangle ΔHEN. Then construct equilateral triangle ΔENX. Continue to construct each of the remaining triangles.

H •———————————————————————————• E

# Chapter 2:
# Kites and Basic Constructions

 DOI: 10.4324/9781003235477-2

# Lesson 2.1
# Construct an Isosceles Triangle and a Kite

A triangle is called **isosceles** when at least two of its sides are the same length. The third side is called the **base**. Follow the directions below to construct isosceles ∆KIT with base $\overline{KT}$ and two sides equal to $\overline{MN}$. Your construction will look like the example to the right.

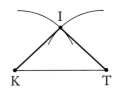

1. Draw a short arc with center M passing through N. This will ensure that the compass radius is set at $\overline{MN}$.

2. Keeping radius MN, draw a long arc with center K, above and to the right of K.

3. Keeping radius MN, draw a long arc with center T, above and to the left of T.

4. Label the point where the arcs cross, I.

5. Draw $\overline{KI}$ and $\overline{TI}$. KI = TI, making ∆KIT isosceles!

M •————————• N

K •————————————————• T

If you draw two isosceles triangles with the same base, then the pairs of equal sides form a **kite**, as shown in the example to the right. Follow the directions below to finish drawing kite KITE, still using $\overline{KT}$ above.

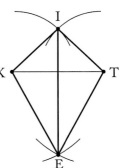

6. Open your compass to a wider radius of your choice.

7. Draw an arc with center K, below and to the right of K.

8. Draw an arc with center T, below and to the left of T.

9. Label the point where the two arcs cross, E.

10. Draw $\overline{KE}$ and $\overline{TE}$. KE = TE, making KITE a kite!

11. Also draw $\overline{IE}$. $\overline{KT}$ and $\overline{IE}$ are called **diagonals** of KITE. A diagonal of a kite is a segment that connects opposite corners.

# Lesson 2.2
## Two Special Kites: A Rhombus and a Non-Convex Kite

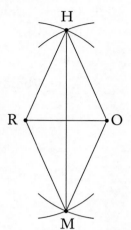

A kite that has four equal sides is called a **rhombus**. Follow the directions below to construct rhombus RHOM, as in the picture to the right.

1. Open your compass to any radius you like. Construct an isosceles triangle above $\overline{RO}$.

2. Construct another isosceles triangle the same size below $\overline{RO}$.

3. Label the top point H and the bottom point M. RHOM is a rhombus.

4. Draw the other diagonal, $\overline{HM}$.

R •————————————• O

Both kites you have drawn so far are **convex**: one isoceles triangle is above and the other is below their common base. If both triangles are on the same side of their common base, the kite is called **nonconvex**. Now you will construct a nonconvex kite.

5. Using any radius you choose, construct an isosceles triangle above base $\overline{KT}$.

6. Change your compass radius, and construct another isosceles triangle—also above base $\overline{KT}$.

7. Label the new corner points I and E.

8. Draw the diagonal $\overline{IE}$.

K •————————————————• T

The diagonals of KITE are $\overline{IE}$ and $\overline{KT}$. Compare the nonconvex kite above with the convex kite you drew on page 10. How are the diagonals of a nonconvex kite different from those of a convex kite?

_____

_____

_____

# Lesson 2.3
# Useful Properties of Kites

As you know, a kite is formed from two isosceles triangles with a common base. These triangles may be tipped sideways, as in the picture to the right. The common base, $\overline{KT}$, is one diagonal of a kite. The other diagonal is called the **main diagonal, $\overline{EI}$.** The main diagonal of a kite has several properties that are used extensively in constructions. See if you can discover them.

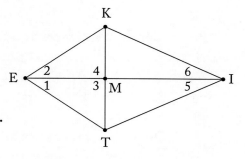

Circle your answers to the following questions:

a.  What type of angle is angle 4: acute, right, or obtuse?

b.  Which length is longer: KM, TM, or are they equal?

c.  Which angle is wider: angle 1, angle 2, or are they equal?

d.  Which angle is wider: angle 5, angle 6, or are they equal?

You may have discovered several properties of the main diagonal of any kite. We will use them often in constructions. Learn them!

1.  The diagonals of a kite are **perpendicular**, because they form right angles. (Did you find that angle 4 is a right angle?)

2.  The main diagonal of a kite contains the **midpoint** of the other diagonal. (Did you find that M was exactly in the middle of $\overline{KT}$?)

3.  The main diagonal is thus the **perpendicular bisector** of the other diagonal. (To *bisect* means "to cut into two equal pieces.")

4.  The main diagonal is the **angle bisector** of each angle. (Did you find that angle 1 was equal to angle 2, and also that angle 5 was equal to angle 6?)

## Lesson 2.4
# Construct the Midpoint of a Segment Using Its Perpendicular Bisector

The **perpendicular bisector** of a segment is a line that contains the midpoint of the segment and is perpendicular to the segment. To construct the perpendicular bisector, simply construct the main diagonal of a kite. Your construction will look like the example to the right.

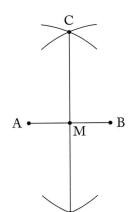

1. Open the compass to any radius greater than half the length of $\overline{AB}$. (An easy radius to use is AB itself.)

2. Draw an arc with center A, above and to the right of A.

3. Keeping the same radius, draw an arc with center B, above and to the left of B.

4. Label the point where the two arcs intersect, C.

5. Draw two more arcs with the same radius (one with center A and the other with center B) that intersect *below* segment $\overline{AB}$. Label this intersection D.

6. Use the straightedge to draw $\overline{CD}$. $\overline{CD}$ is the **perpendicular bisector** of $\overline{AB}$.

7. The point where $\overline{CD}$ crosses $\overline{AB}$ is the **midpoint** of $\overline{AB}$. Label it M.

A •————————————• B

8. On the picture in the upper right corner of the page, lightly draw all four sides of kite ACBD; $\overline{CD}$ is its main diagonal.

# Lesson 2.5
## Construct a Square When Given Its Diagonal

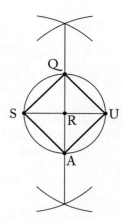

A **square** is a special type of kite that has four equal sides and four equal angles. The four corners of a square lie on a circle. See the example to the right.

Using $\overline{SU}$ below as a diagonal, construct a square following the directions below.

1. Construct the perpendicular bisector of $\overline{SU}$. (Follow the procedure you learned in Lesson 2.4.)

2. Label the midpoint of $\overline{SU}$, R.

3. Draw a circle with center R and passing through S.

4. Label the points where the circle crosses the perpendicular bisector, Q and A.

5. Use your straightedge to draw $\overline{SQ}$, $\overline{UQ}$, $\overline{SA}$, and $\overline{UA}$. SQUA is a square!

S •————————————————• U

Name_____    Date_____

# Lesson 2.6
# Bisect an Angle

An **angle** is made up of two rays with a common endpoint. The rays are called the **sides** of the angle. The endpoint is called the **vertex** of the angle. We often use the vertex point to name the angle; for example, the angle in the middle of this page called "angle B."

    To **bisect** an angle means to draw a ray that splits the angle into two equal angles. The ray is called an **angle bisector.** Our angle bisector will be the main diagonal of a kite. Follow the directions below to bisect angle B.

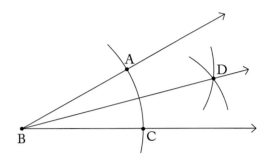

1. Draw an arc with center B and a radius of your choice, but not too small. Label the points where the arc crosses each side of the angle, A and C.

2. Draw an arc with center A.

3. With the same radius, draw an arc with center C.

4. Label the point where the two arcs cross, D.

5. Draw a ray from B through D. This ray bisects angle B. (Imagine drawing $\overline{AD}$ and $\overline{CD}$. Do you see that BADC would be a kite?)

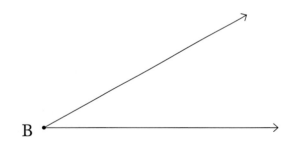

B

6. Now, use the same procedure to bisect right angle P below.

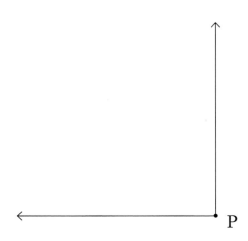

P

# Lesson 2.7
# Construct a Regular Octagon

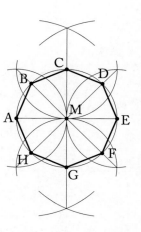

A **regular octagon** has eight equal sides and eight equal angles. Like a square, all of the corners of a regular octagon lie on a circle. Your construction will look like the one to the right.

1. Construct the perpendicular bisector of $\overline{AE}$. (Remember Lesson 2.4?)

2. Label the midpoint of $\overline{AE}$, M.

3. Draw a circle with center M and passing through A.

4. Label the points where the circle crosses the perpendicular bisector, C and G.

*Note*: The point M is the vertex of four right angles. One of them has sides $\overrightarrow{MA}$ and $\overrightarrow{MC}$. In steps 5–7, you will construct the angle bisector of this right angle.

5. Draw a long arc with center A and passing through M.

6. Draw a long arc with center C and passing through M. Be sure that the two arcs cross. (Do you see that this crossing point, and A, M, and C, are corners of a kite?)

7. Draw the angle bisector from M through the intersection of those two arcs.

8. Label the point where the circle with center M intersects the angle bisector, B.

9. Use the method of steps 5–8 to construct the angle bisectors of each of the other three right angles with vertex M. (You will construct a 4-petal flower, too; if you wish, color in the petals with colored pencils!)

10. Label the points where the circle with center M intersects these angle bisectors, D, F, and H.

11. Connect the eight points on the circle to form regular octagon ABCDEFGH.

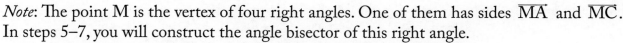

A •————————————————————• E

# Lesson 2.8
## Construct a Regular Dodecagon (Clock)

Look back at the construction of a regular octagon in Lesson 2.7. Ignore the angle bisectors, ignore the points B, D, F, and H, and ignore the octagon. Can you see how the arcs you drew form four petals of a flower? Can you see how to draw those petals using just four long arcs? These arcs, together with the vertical and horizontal line segments, cross the circle with center M in 12 equally spaced points. These points form the vertices of a regular dodecagon.

On segment $\overline{AG}$ below, recreate the construction of the four petals. Omit the angle bisectors, and omit the octagon. Locate the 12 points equally spaced around the circle, and construct a **regular dodecagon**—a polygon with 12 equal sides and 12 angles. Decorate your dodecagon with the numbers of a clock (1–12).

A  G

# Chapter 3:
# Centers of a Triangle

DOI: 10.4324/9781003235477-3

# Lesson 3.1
# Drop a Perpendicular

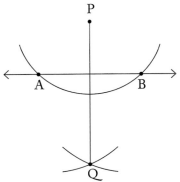

Imagine dropping a ball onto the floor. The ball will fall in a line that is perpendicular to the floor. In the diagram, point P represents the ball, and the given line represents the floor. Through point P, we will construct a line that is perpendicular to the given line. This perpendicular will be the main diagonal of a kite.

1. Open the compass to any convenient radius that is greater than the distance between P and the line.

2. Draw an arc with center P that crosses the line in two points. Label these points A and B. (Imagine connecting $\overline{PA}$ and $\overline{PB}$ to form an isosceles triangle.)

3. Draw an arc with center A, below and to the right of A.

4. Keeping the same radius, draw another arc with center B, below and to the left of B.

5. Label the point where the two arcs cross, Q.

6. Draw $\overline{PQ}$, which is perpendicular to the line.

7. On the sample diagram above, draw kite PBQA. Do you see that $\overline{PQ}$ is the main diagonal of kite PBQA?

P •

# Lesson 3.2
## Centers of a Triangle I: Altitudes

In any triangle, if you drop a perpendicular from a vertex to the opposite side, the segment you construct is called an **altitude**. The altitudes from A and from B are shown in the sample diagram to the right. The altitude from C is not shown.

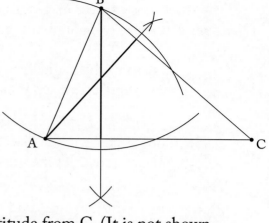

1. Drop a perpendicular from B to $\overline{AC}$. This is the altitude from B. (Use the method shown in Lesson 3.1.)

2. Drop a perpendicular from A to $\overline{BC}$. This is the altitude from A.

3. Drop a perpendicular from C to $\overline{AB}$. This is the altitude from C. (It is not shown in the sample diagram, but you can construct it using the same method.)

4. If you have worked very carefully, the three altitudes should intersect at a single point. (If they don't, find your mistake and fix it!) Label that point the **orthocenter**. (*Ortho-* means "right" or "straight." For example, an orthodontist straightens teeth. Because altitudes intersect sides at right angles, the intersection point of the altitudes is called the orthocenter.)

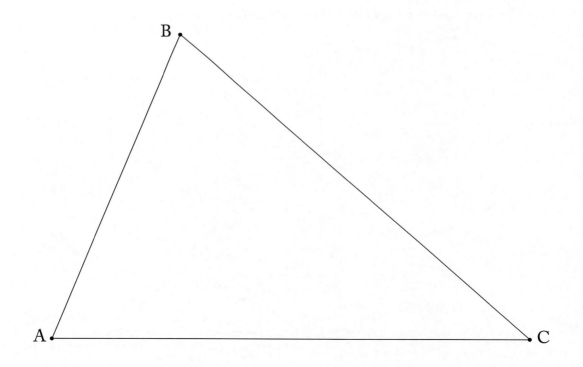

# Lesson 3.3
# Centers of a Triangle II: Angle Bisectors

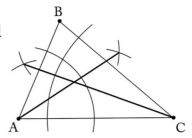

The three angle bisectors of a triangle also meet at one point, called the **incenter**. The angle bisectors from A and from C are shown at right.

1. Construct the angle bisector of angle A. (Use the method shown in Lesson 2.6.)

2. Construct the angle bisector of angle C.

3. Construct the angle bisector of angle B. (It is not shown in the sample picture, but you can construct it using the same method.)

4. If you have worked very carefully, all three angle bisectors should meet at a single point. (If they don't, find your mistake and fix it!) Label this point the **incenter**. (It is the center of the **inscribed circle**, which you will draw in steps 5 and 6.)

5. Drop a perpendicular from the incenter to side $\overline{AC}$. Label the point where this perpendicular crosses $\overline{AC}$, P. (This construction is shown at left. Use the method shown in Lesson 3.1.)

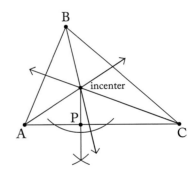

6. Draw the circle with center at the incenter and passing through P. This circle should just touch all three sides of the triangle. (*Scribe* means "to write" or "to draw." The **inscribed circle** is drawn inside the triangle.)

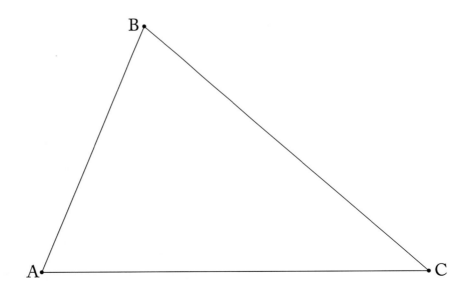

# Lesson 3.4
# Centers of a Triangle III: Perpendicular Bisectors

1. Construct the **perpendicular bisector** of $\overline{BC}$, as shown in the example to the right. (Use the method shown in Lesson 2.4.)

2. Using the same method, construct the perpendicular bisectors of sides $\overline{AB}$ and $\overline{AC}$.

3. The three perpendicular bisectors should meet at a single point. (If they don't, find your mistake and fix it!) Label this point the **circumcenter**. (It is the center of the **circumscribed circle**.)

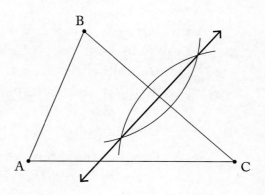

4. Draw the circle with center at the circumcenter and passing through A. *This circle should pass through points A, B, and C.* (*Circum-* means "around." For example, Magellan's expedition circumnavigated, or sailed around, the world. The **circumscribed circle** is drawn around the triangle.)

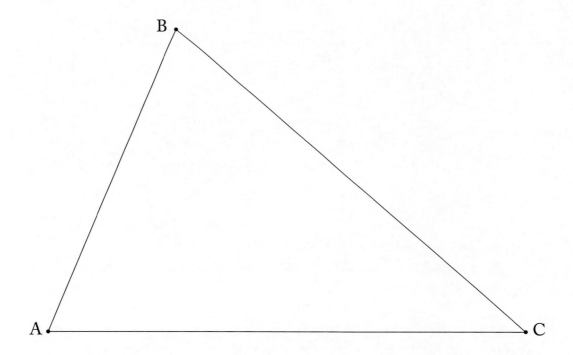

# Lesson 3.5
# Centers of a Triangle IV: Medians

A **median** of a triangle is a segment that connects a vertex to the midpoint of the opposite side.

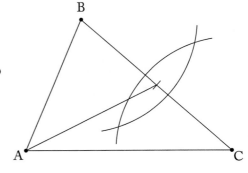

1. In ΔABC below, construct the **midpoint** of side $\overline{BC}$. (To do this, construct its perpendicular bisector—but make it *very short*, just long enough to cross $\overline{BC}$ and locate its midpoint.)

2. Use the straightedge to connect the midpoint to its opposite vertex. This segment is a **median** (as shown at right).

3. Using the same method, construct the other two medians of ΔABC.

4. The three medians should intersect in a single point. (If they don't, find your mistake and fix it!) Label this point the **centroid**.

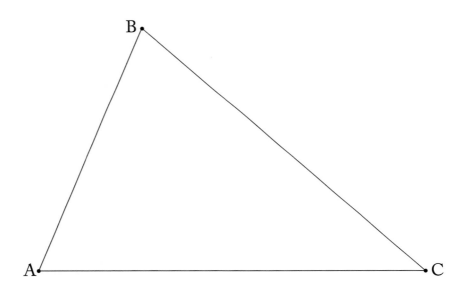

The centroid splits each median into two parts, one short and one long. How much longer is the long part? To answer this question, choose any one of the medians, and open your compass radius to the size of its short part. Exactly how many short parts will fit into the long part? _____

Extra Credit: Obtain a piece of cardboard, draw any triangle on it, locate its centroid, and cut out the triangle. It will balance at its centroid on the tip of a pin!

# Lesson 3.6
# The Nine-Point Circle

If you enjoyed constructing the orthocenter, circumcenter, and centroid, then you may enjoy the challenge of putting them into the same picture.

1.  In ΔABC below, construct all three **altitudes**, and label the orthocenter, O.

2.  Construct all three **perpendicular bisectors**, and label the circumcenter, Ci.

3.  Construct all three **medians**, and label the centroid, Ce.

4.  Draw the segment $\overline{OCi}$ connecting the orthocenter and the circumcenter. (If you have worked very carefully, the centroid, Ce, will lie on this segment.)

5.  Open your compass radius to the length CiCe.

a.  How many of these lengths will fit into the segment $\overline{OCe}$? _____

6.  Construct the midpoint of the segment $\overline{OCi}$. Label it M.

7.  Construct a circle with center M and passing through the midpoint of any side. This is called the **Nine-Point Circle**.

b.  Find and list all nine interesting points that it passes through. (There are three types, each with three points.)

_____

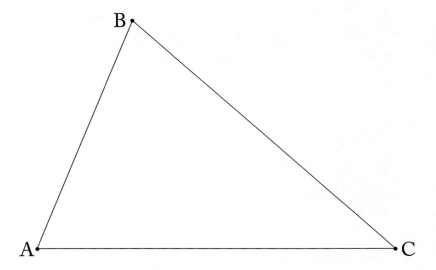

# Chapter 4:
# Perpendiculars
# and Rectangles

DOI: 10.4324/9781003235477-4

# Lesson 4.1
# Erect a Perpendicular

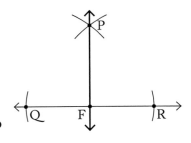

In Lesson 3.1, you learned to drop a perpendicular from an external point to a given line. You used this method to construct the altitudes of triangles. It also is possible to erect a perpendicular from a point *on* a given line, like F on the segment below. We will use the fact that *two points equidistant from the endpoints of a segment determine its perpendicular bisector*. In the example to the right, F and Q are the two equidistant points.

1. First, use your straightedge to make the segment below longer.

2. Using any convenient radius (not too short), construct two arcs with center F crossing the segment on opposite sides of the center. Label the crossing points, Q and R. (Note that F is equidistant from Q and R.)

3. Using any longer radius, construct an arc above F with center Q.

4. Using the same radius, construct an arc with center R above F.

5. Label the point where these two arcs cross, P. (Note that P is also equidistant from Q and R.)

6. Draw $\overleftrightarrow{PF}$. $\overleftrightarrow{PF}$ is the perpendicular bisector of $\overline{QR}$. F is called the **foot** of this perpendicular.

Can you imagine $\overleftrightarrow{PF}$ as the main diagonal of a kite?

—————————————•——————————————————————
              F

Name_____     Date_____

# Lesson 4.2
# Construct a Parallel Line I: Using a Perpendicular

**Parallel** lines never meet. Through the point P below, we can construct a line that is parallel to line *l*. We will use the theorem that *two lines perpendicular to the same line are parallel.*

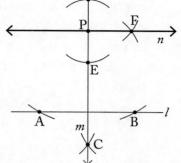

1. Drop a perpendicular from P to line *l*. (To do this, draw two arcs with center P that cross *l* at A and B. Draw two more arcs with centers A and B that intersect at C below the lines. Draw $\overline{PC}$.) Extend $\overline{PC}$ above P.

2. Erect a line through P perpendicular to $\overline{PC}$. (To do this, draw two arcs with center P that cross $\overline{PC}$ at D and E. Draw two arcs with centers D and E that intersect at F. Draw $\overleftrightarrow{PF}$.)

3. Lines *l* and $\overleftrightarrow{PF}$ are parallel, because they are both perpendicular to $\overline{PC}$.

. P

_____ *l*

# Lesson 4.3
## Construct a Rectangle When Given Two Sides I

A **rectangle** is a quadrilateral with four right angles. You can construct a rectangle by erecting perpendiculars. (You learned how to erect a perpendicular in Lesson 4.1.)

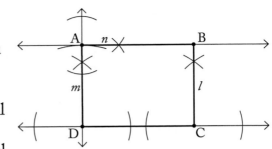

Build your rectangle on side $\overline{CD}$ below. Make the shorter sides the same length as $\overline{QP}$. The construction will look like the picture at right.

1. Erect a line through D perpendicular to $\overline{CD}$. Label the line, *m*.

2. Open your compass radius to the length QP. Make an arc with center D, above D. Label the point where the arc crosses line *m*, A.

3. Erect a line through A perpendicular to *m*. Label the line, *n*.

4. Erect a line through C perpendicular to $\overline{CD}$. Label the line, *l*.

5. Label the point where *l* crosses *n*, B. Then ABCD is a rectangle, because all of its sides are perpendicular.

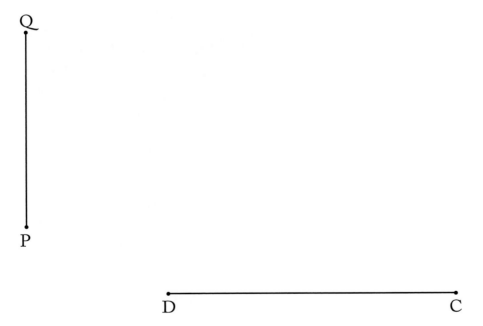

$\overline{AB}$ and $\overline{CD}$ are **opposite sides** of rectangle ABCD. $\overline{BC}$ and $\overline{DA}$ also are opposite sides.

In what two ways are opposite sides of a rectangle related to each other?

_____

_____

# Lesson 4.4
## Construct a Rectangle When Given Two Sides II

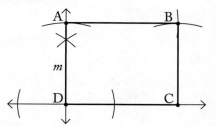

Opposite sides of a rectangle are equal in length. This property provides a quicker way to construct a rectangle. First construct one right angle, and then make all of the sides the correct lengths. Your construction will look like the drawing on the right.

1. Erect a line through D perpendicular to $\overline{CD}$. Label the line, *m*.

2. Open your compass radius to the length QP. Make an arc with center D, above D. Label the point where the arc crosses line *m*, A.

3. Keeping the same radius QP, make an arc with center C, above C.

4. Change the radius to DC, and make an arc with center A, to the right of A.

5. Label the point where these arcs cross, B.

6. Draw $\overline{AB}$ and $\overline{BC}$. ABCD is a rectangle, because its opposite sides are equal and it has a right angle.

Q

P

D                                                                 C

Now, draw the diagonals of rectangle ABCD.

In what two ways are the diagonals of a rectangle related to each other?

_____

_____

# Lesson 4.5
## Construct a Square When Given Its Side

A **square** is a special type of rectangle in which all four sides are the same length. In Lesson 2.5, you constructed a square given its *diagonal*. Now, use what you have learned about rectangles to construct a square given its *side*. Build your square on side $\overline{DC}$ below. Show all of the construction arcs you need—don't erase them!

a. Describe each step of your construction.

1. Erect a line through D perpendicular to $\overline{CD}$. Label the line, *m*.

2. _____

3. _____

4. _____

5. _____

6. _____

7. _____

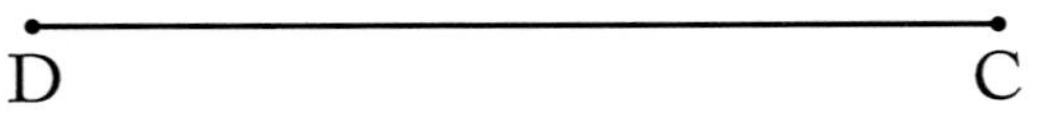

D                                    C

Draw the diagonals of square ABCD.

b. In what four ways are the diagonals of a square related to each other (or to the angles of the square)?

_____

_____

# Chapter 5:
# Parallels and Parallelograms

DOI: 10.4324/9781003235477-5

Name_____     Date_____

# Lesson 5.1
# Copy an Angle

To copy an angle means to construct an angle with the same measure but located somewhere else. You will copy angle A onto the line below. The finished construction will look like the drawing on the right.

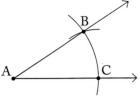

1. Open your compass to any convenient radius.

2. Draw an arc with center A that crosses both sides of angle A. Label the points where the arc crosses the sides of the angle, B and C, with B above C.

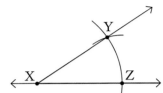

3. Keeping the same radius, draw an arc with center X. Make the arc about the same length as the arc you drew in step 2. Label the point where the arc crosses the working line, Z.

4. Draw a short arc with center C passing through B, so that the radius of the compass is the length BC.

5. Keeping the radius BC, draw an arc with center Z. Label the point where the two arcs cross, Y.

6. Draw $\overrightarrow{XY}$.

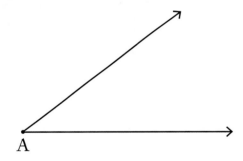

A

X

Angle YXZ is a copy of angle BAC. We also say that angle YXZ is **congruent** to angle BAC. In symbols, we write $\angle YXZ \cong \angle BAC$.

# Lesson 5.2
# Construct a Parallel Line II: Using an Oblique Line

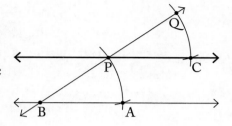

This construction shows that you don't need perpendiculars to construct parallels. We will use an **oblique** line $\overleftrightarrow{PB}$. (An oblique line is neither perpendicular nor parallel to a given line.)

To construct a parallel line through P, you will copy the angle with vertex B to a corresponding position with vertex P. The construction will look like the picture at right.

1. Draw an arc with center B and passing through P. Label the point where the arc crosses the horizontal line, A.

2. Keeping the same radius, draw an arc with center P that crosses the oblique line above P and curves to the right. Label the point where the arc crosses the oblique line, Q.

3. Change the radius so you can draw an arc with center P that passes through A.

4. Keeping the radius PA, draw an arc with center Q that crosses the other arc with center P. Label the point where the arcs cross, C.

5. Draw $\overleftrightarrow{PC}$, which is parallel to the horizontal line. (Do you see that you have copied angle B?)

6. To see why these lines are parallel, observe that $\angle PBA$ is congruent to $\angle QPC$. *If corresponding angles are congruent, then lines are parallel.*

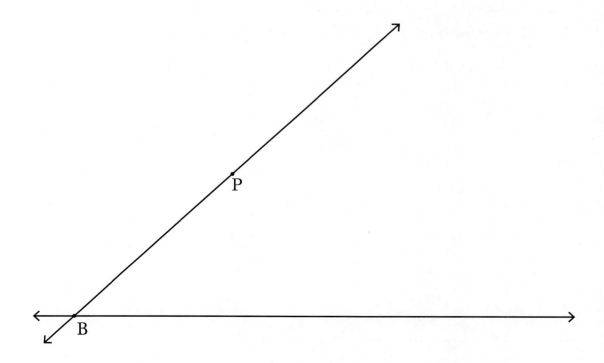

# Lesson 5.3
## Construct a Parallelogram I: Using the Definition

By definition, a **parallelogram** is a quadrilateral in which both pairs of opposite sides are parallel. Use point P and side $\overline{SR}$ below to construct a parallelogram. The construction will look like to the one on the right.

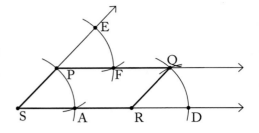

1. Draw ray $\overrightarrow{SP}$ (which includes side $\overline{SP}$). Also extend ray $\overrightarrow{SR}$ to the right.

2. Open your compass to the radius $\overline{SP}$. Draw an arc with center S and passing through P. Label the point where this arc crosses $\overrightarrow{SR}$, A.

3. Keeping the same radius, draw an arc with center P, about the same size. Label the point where this arc crosses $\overrightarrow{SP}$, E.

4. Keeping the same radius, draw an arc with center R, about the same size. Label the point where this arc crosses $\overrightarrow{SR}$, D.

5. Change your compass radius to PA. Draw an arc with center E. Label the point where this arc crosses the arc with center P, F. (Do you see that you are copying angle S?)

6. Draw the line $\overleftrightarrow{PF}$, which will be parallel to $\overrightarrow{SR}$, because *if corresponding angles are congruent, then lines are parallel.*

7. Keeping the radius PA, draw an arc with center D that crosses the arc with center R. If all has gone well, this arc will cross the parallel line at the same point. Label this point Q. Draw $\overline{RQ}$. (Do you see that $\angle QRD$ is a copy of angle S?) Because corresponding angles are congruent, $\overline{RQ}$ is parallel to $\overline{SP}$.

8. Because both pairs of opposite sides are parallel, PQRS is a parallelogram by the definition.

$\bullet$ P

S $\bullet$————————————————$\bullet$ R

# Lesson 5.4
## Discerning Properties of Parallelograms

Look back at parallelogram PQRS you constructed in Lesson 5.3. Answer the following questions about it by circling the appropriate responses.

a.  $\overline{PS}$ and $\overline{QR}$ are called **opposite sides**. $\overline{PQ}$ and $\overline{SR}$ also are opposite sides. Are these pairs of opposite sides parallel?

   Yes   No

b.  Segments that have the same length are called **congruent**. Are opposite sides in parallelogram PQRS congruent?

   Yes   No

c.  Do you think opposite sides of *any* parallelogram would be congruent? (*Hint*: Think about drawing the arc with center R in Step 4.)

   Yes   No

d.  In PQRS, angles PSR and RQP are called **opposite angles**. Angles QPS and SRQ are also opposite angles. Are opposite angles congruent?

   Yes   No

e.  Do you think opposite angles of *any* parallelogram would be congruent?

   Yes   No

f.  Angles PSR and QRS and are called **consecutive angles**. What relationship do consecutive angles have to each other? (*Hint:* Remember that $\angle PSR \cong \angle QRD$ .)

   i. Consecutive angles are congruent.
   ii. Consecutive angles are supplementary (their sum is 180°).
   iii. Consecutive angles are complementary (their sum is 90°).

Now, turn back to your construction in Lesson 5.3 and draw the diagonals $\overline{SQ}$ and $\overline{PR}$. Answer the following questions by circling the appropriate responses.

g.  Are the diagonals of PQRS congruent?

   Yes   No

h.  Are the diagonals of PQRS perpendicular to each other?

   Yes   No

i.  Do the diagonals of PQRS bisect its angles?

   Yes   No

j.  Do the diagonals of PQRS bisect each other?

   Yes   No

# Lesson 5.5
## Construct a Parallelogram II: An Easier Way

One geometry theorem states that, *if two sides of a quadrilateral are both parallel and congruent, then it is a parallelogram.* This fact implies an easier way to construct a parallelogram.

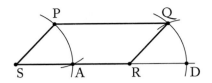

Use point P and side $\overline{SR}$ below. You will construct $\overline{RQ}$ both parallel and congruent to $\overline{SP}$.

1. Draw ray $\overline{SR}$ (which includes side $\overline{SR}$). Draw ray $\overline{SP}$.

2. Draw an arc with radius SP and center S. Label the point where this arc crosses $\overline{SR}$, A.

3. Keeping the same radius, draw an arc with center R to the right of R. Label the point where this arc crosses $\overline{SR}$, D.

4. Open your compass radius to PA. Draw an arc with center D that crosses the arc with center R. Label the point where these arcs cross, Q. Draw $\overline{RQ}$ and $\overline{PQ}$.

5. Because $\overline{PS}$ is parallel and congruent to $\overline{QR}$, PQRS is a parallelogram.


•
P




•
S                                                    •
                                                     R

# Lesson 5.6
# Construct a Parallelogram III: The Easiest Way

Yet another geometry theorem states that, *if both pairs of opposite sides of a quadrilateral are congruent, then it is a parallelogram.* Show how to use this theorem to construct parallelogram PQRS below. Describe each step of your construction. (Hint: You only need to draw two arcs to locate point Q.)

1. _____

2. _____

3. _____

4. _____

• P

S •_____• R

# Chapter 6:
# Constructing Triangles

 DOI: 10.4324/9781003235477-6

# Lesson 6.1
# Construct a Triangle Given SSS

Suppose you are given three lengths. Can you construct a triangle using those lengths as its three sides? In other words, given **Side-Side-Side (SSS)**, can you construct a triangle? Could you construct two different triangles using the same three sides? If three given sides can be used to construct one and only one triangle, then we will say that **SSS determines a triangle**. But, does it matter how long the sides are?

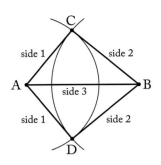

Below are three side lengths, side 1, side 2, and side 3. We will build triangles above and below side 3. The finished construction will look like the picture at right.

1. Open your compass radius to be the length of side 1.

2. Keeping that radius, draw a big arc—half of a circle—with center A and radius side 1. The arc should cross $\overline{AB}$.

3. Open your compass radius to be the length of side 2.

4. Draw a big arc with center B and radius side 2.

5. Label the points where the two arcs cross, C and D.

6. Draw $\overline{AC}$ and $\overline{BC}$, and label them side 1 and side 2.

7. Draw $\overline{AD}$ and $\overline{BD}$, and also label them side 1 and side 2.

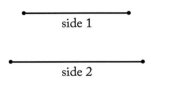

side 1

side 2

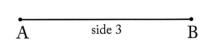

A          side 3          B

a. Using your imagination, how could you move ΔABC to fit on top of ΔABD?

_____

_____

b. Do ΔABC and ΔABD have the same size and shape? _____

c. In this case, does SSS determine a triangle? _____

8. Suppose we make side 3 a little longer. Use the SSS method to construct △ABE with these three side lengths. Make just one triangle, either above or below $\overline{AB}$.

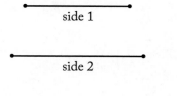

side 1

side 2

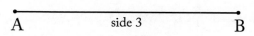

A        side 3        B

d. For this obtuse triangle, does SSS determine a triangle? _____

9. Now let's make side 3 even longer. Try to construct a triangle with these three side lengths:

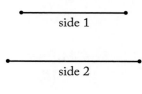

side 1

side 2

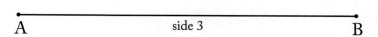

A        side 3        B

e. What went wrong?

_____

_____

f. In order to be able to construct a triangle, how must the length of side 3 be related to the lengths of the two shorter sides?

_____

_____

g. Given three sides that fit this restriction, will SSS determine a triangle? _____

# Lesson 6.2
# Using SSS to Copy a Triangle Into Kites or Parallelograms

Follow these directions to create a copy of ΔPQR flipped over side $\overline{PR}$.
1. Draw an arc with center P and radius PQ on the left side of ΔPQR.

2. Draw an arc with center R and radius RQ on the left side of ΔPQR.

3. Label the point where the arcs intersect, S.

4. Draw segments $\overline{PS}$ and $\overline{RS}$.

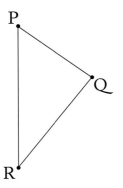

a. What special type of quadrilateral is PQRS? _____

Construct three copies of the triangle below, flipping it over each side. You will draw six arcs. Each side is the radius of two arcs, one centered at each endpoint. The finished construction should look like the picture at right.

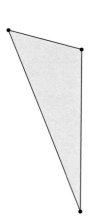

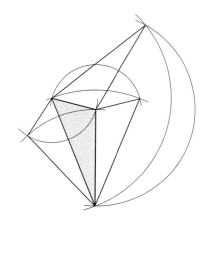

b. How many kites are in your construction? _____

Follow the directions below to create a copy of △PQR that has been rotated around the midpoint of side $\overline{PR}$.

1. Use radius QR to draw an arc with center P (!) on the left side of △PQR.

2. Switch to radius QP to draw an arc with center R (!) on the left side of △PQR.

3. Label the point where the arcs intersect, T.

4. Draw segments $\overline{PT}$ and $\overline{RT}$.

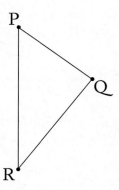

c.  What special type of quadrilateral is PQRT? _____

Construct three copies of the triangle below, rotating it around the midpoint of each side. You will draw three circles. Each side is the radius of one circle with its center being the opposite vertex. The finished construction should look like the picture at right.

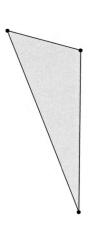

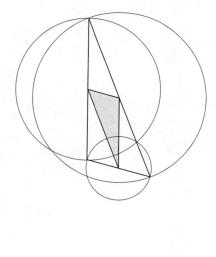

d.  How many parallelograms are in your construction? _____

**Lesson 6.2, Continued**

Reconsider your construction as one large white triangle with a small grey triangle inside. Each side of the grey triangle is called a **midsegment** of the large white triangle, because each side of the grey triangle connects the midpoints of two sides of the white triangle.

> e. How does the length of each midsegment compare with the length of the side that it is parallel to?
>
> _____
>
> f. How does the area of the inner triangle compare with the area of the outer triangle?
>
> _____

Again reconsider your construction. The three circles shown in the picture intersect in three other points that were not used to form the parallelograms. Redraw those three circles below. Connect one of these other intersection points to the two nearest vertices of the grey triangle.

> g. What kind of special quadrilateral is formed? _____

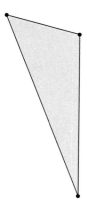

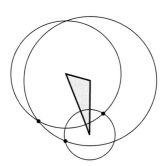

# Lesson 6.3
## Using SSS to Copy an Angle

This lesson verifies the method of Lesson 5.1. To copy an angle means to construct an angle with the same measure but located somewhere else. You will copy angle A onto the line below. The finished construction will look like the one on the right.

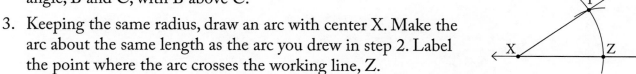

1. Open your compass to any convenient radius.

2. Draw an arc with center A that crosses both sides of angle A. Label the points where the arc crosses the sides of the angle, B and C, with B above C.

3. Keeping the same radius, draw an arc with center X. Make the arc about the same length as the arc you drew in step 2. Label the point where the arc crosses the working line, Z.

4. Draw a short arc with center C passing through B, so that the radius of the compass is the length BC.

5. Keeping the radius BC, draw an arc with center Z. Label the point where the two arcs cross, Y.

6. Draw $\overline{XY}$.

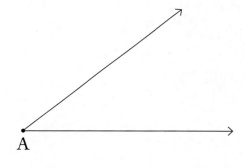

How can we be sure that angle YXZ is a copy of angle BAC? Because SSS determines a triangle, $\triangle YXZ$ and $\triangle BAC$ must have the same size and shape. Hence corresponding angles must have the same measure, so $\angle YXZ \cong \angle BAC$.

# Lesson 6.4
# Construct a Triangle Given ASA

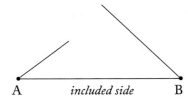

The picture at left shows another way to think about constructing a triangle. Given a side and the two angles that fit on either end, can you construct one and only one triangle? In other words, does **Angle-Side-Angle (ASA)** determine a triangle? (The given side is "included" because it is a part of each angle.)

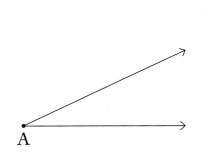

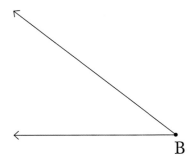

You will fit copies of angles A and B onto each endpoint of side $\overline{AB}$ below. The construction will look like the picture at right.

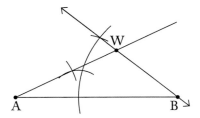

1. Copy angle A onto the left endpoint of $\overline{AB}$. (Use the method found in Lesson 6.3.)

2. Copy angle B onto the right endpoint of $\overline{AB}$.

3. Label the point where the rays cross, W. You have created Δ ABW.

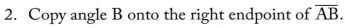

4. Here is an obtuse angle C that replaces angle A. Copy angle B onto the right endpoint of $\overline{CB}$ below to create ΔCBV.

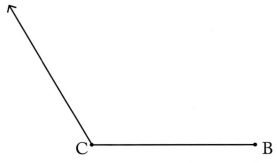

5. Here is a copy of angle C from the previous page, but a different angle B. Copy this angle B onto the right endpoint of $\overline{CB}$.

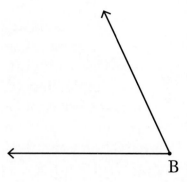

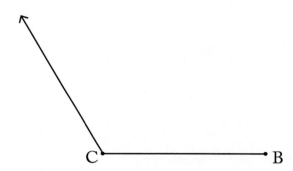

a. Why can't you construct ΔCBV in this case?

_____

_____

b. Does the length of the given side $\overline{CB}$ make any difference? _____

c. If the two given angles can belong to the same triangle, then their sum must be smaller than what number? _____

d. Given two angles that fit the restriction in question C, and the side included between them, will ASA determine a triangle? _____

# Lesson 6.5
## Construct a Triangle Given SAS

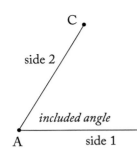

The picture at left indicates yet another possible way to construct a triangle. Suppose you are given two sides and the angle included between them. Can you construct one and only one triangle? In other words, does **Side-Angle-Side (SAS)** determine a triangle? Your finished construction will look like the picture at right.

1.  Copy side 1 onto the horizontal side of angle A; label the intersection point B.

2.  Copy side 2 onto the oblique side of angle A; label the intersection point C.

3.  Draw $\overline{BC}$.

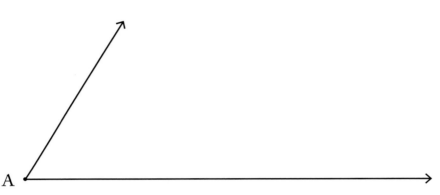

4.  Now copy side 1 onto the *oblique* side of ∠A; label the intersection point D.

5.  Copy side 2 onto the *horizontal* side of ∠A; label the intersection point E.

6.  Draw $\overline{DE}$.

a.  Does △ABC have the same size and shape as △ADE? _____

7.  Now copy side 1 and side 2 onto this obtuse angle to form a triangle.

b. Does SAS determine a triangle even if the angle is obtuse? _____

c. Would it matter if the sides were longer or shorter? _____

d. Does SAS always determine a triangle? _____

# Lesson 6.6
# When Does SSA Determine a Triangle

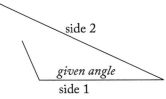

side 2

*given angle*

side 1

Suppose you are given an angle, a side adjacent to the angle (side 1), and a side opposite the angle (side 2). Does **Side-Side-Angle (SSA)** determine a triangle? The answer depends on the type of angle and on the relative lengths of the two sides. We investigate eight cases, first with an obtuse angle, then with a right angle, then with an acute angle.

**Case I.** The angle is obtuse, and side 2 is greater than side 1.
1. Open your compass to the radius side 2, and make an arc with center B.
2. Label the point where the arc crosses the oblique side of angle A, C.
3. Draw $\overline{BC}$. Label it side 2.

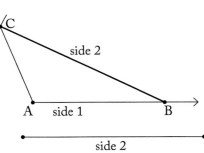

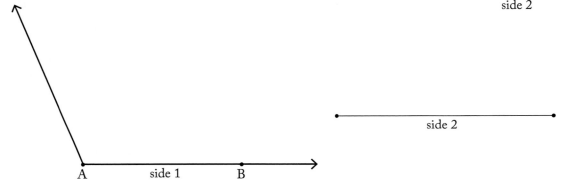

side 2

a. Did SSA determine a triangle in this case? _____

b. If side 2 were longer, would SSA determine a triangle? _____

**Case II.** The angle is obtuse, and side 2 is less than (or equal to) side 1.
4. Open your compass to the radius side 2, and make an arc with center B.

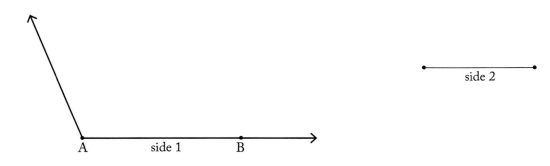

side 2

c. How could you change the length of side 2 to be able to construct a triangle?

_____

d. Why would SsA be a good way to describe the construction method you investigated in Case I and Case II? (In your answer, refer to side 2 as "the side opposite the angle" and refer to side 1 as "the side adjacent to the angle.")

_____

**Case III.** The angle is a right angle.

5. Choose any length for side 2 greater than side 1, and construct a triangle.

6. Choose any length for side 2 less than side 1, and try to construct a triangle.

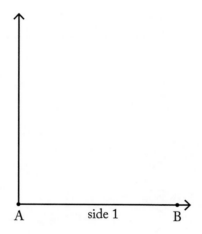

A          side 1          B

e. If side 2 > side 1 and the angle is a right angle, does SsA determine a triangle?

_____

f. Let sSA mean side 2 < side 1. Would sSA ever determine a triangle when the angle is an obtuse or a right angle?

_____

g. Let ssA mean side 2 = side 1. Would ssA ever determine a triangle when the angle is an obtuse or a right angle?

_____

**Case IV.** The angle is acute and side 2 is greater than side 1.

    7.  Make an arc with center B and radius side 2.

    8.  Label the point where this arc crosses the oblique side of angle A, C.

    9.  Draw side $\overline{BC}$.

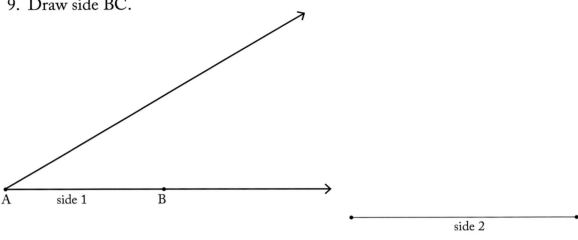

    h.  Would anyone else get the same triangle you did? _____

  10.  Open your compass to any other length of side 2 that is greater than side 1. Try to construct a triangle following steps 7–9.

    i.  If the angle is acute and side 2 > side 1, does SsA determine a triangle? _____

**Case V.** The angle is acute, and side 2 is equal to side 1.

  11.  Open your compass so its radius is the same as side 2.

  12.  Make an arc with center B and radius side 2. Label the point where this arc crosses the oblique side of angle A, C.

  13.  Draw side $\overline{BC}$.

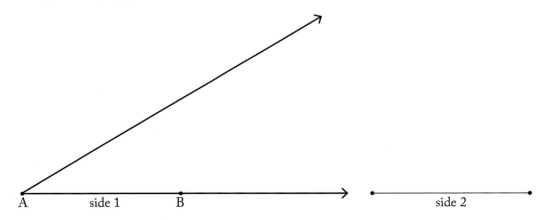

    j.  If the angle is acute, does ssA determine a triangle? _____

**Case VI.** The angle is acute, and side 2 is somewhat shorter than side 1.

14. Open your compass so its radius is the same as side 2.

15. Make an arc with center B and radius side 2.

16. Label the two (!) points where this arc crosses the oblique side of angle A, C and D.

17. Draw sides $\overline{BC}$ and $\overline{BD}$.

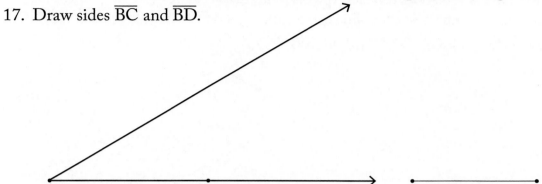

k. How many triangles have you drawn that use angle A, side 1, and this side 2? _____

l. Does sSA determine one and only one triangle in this case? _____

18. Change your radius to be slightly smaller than side 2, and repeat steps 15–17. Change your radius again to be slightly smaller, and repeat steps 15–17.

m. Can you find just the right radius so that points C and D are in the same place? _____

**Case VII.** Side 2 is just short enough to reach the oblique side of angle A.

19. Open your compass so its radius is the same as given side 2, which was carefully chosen to be just the right size.

20. Make an arc with center B and radius side 2.

21. This arc should touch the oblique side of angle A in just one point; label that point C.

22. Draw side $\overline{BC}$.

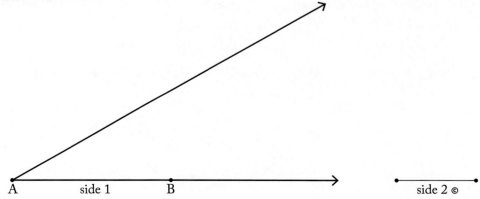

Taylor & Francis • *Hands-On Geometry: Constructions With a Straightedge and Compass*

**Lesson 6.6, Continued**

> n. What kind of angle is angle C? _____
>
> o. Does sSA determine a triangle in this special case? _____

**Case VIII.** Side 2 is too short to reach the oblique side of angle A.

23. Open your compass so its radius is the same as side 2.

24. Make an arc with center B and radius side 2.

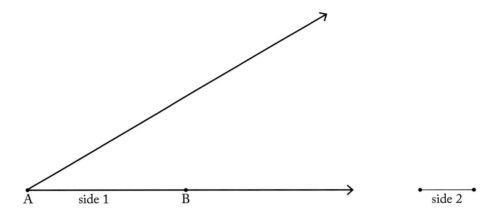

> p. Does the arc cross the oblique side of angle A? _____
>
> q. Does sSA determine a triangle in this case? _____

**Summary of Cases**

> r. These are the three conditions under which SSA determines a triangle:
>
>   i. If **opposite side > adjacent side,** for what kinds of given angles does **SsA** determine a triangle? (*Circle all that apply.*)     obtuse    right    acute
>
>   ii. If **opposite side = adjacent side,** for what kind of given angle does **ssA** determine a triangle? (*Circle one.*)     obtuse    right    acute
>
>   iii. If **opposite side < adjacent side,** for what kind of given angle *might* **sSA** determine a triangle? (*Circle one.*)     obtuse    right    acute
>
>   iv. If sSA does determine a triangle in condition iii, what type of triangle must it be? _____

# Chapter 7:
# The Infinitesimal
# and the Golden Ratio

Name_____          Date_____

# Lesson 7.1
# Construct a Midsegment and Discern Its Properties

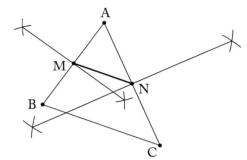

In earlier lessons, you constructed the midpoints of the sides of a triangle. In this lesson, you will connect two of those midpoints with a segment—the **midsegment**—and discern its properties.

1. In the space below, locate any three noncollinear points A, B, and C wherever you choose. Connect them to be the vertices of $\triangle ABC$.

2. Use the perpendicular bisector construction (described in Lesson 2.4) to find the midpoints of $\overline{AB}$ and $\overline{AC}$. Label them M and N.

3. Draw $\overline{MN}$.

Find two interesting relationships between $\overline{MN}$ and $\overline{BC}$.

_____

_____

# Lesson 7.2
# Join the Midpoints of Any Quadrilateral

The midpoints of the sides of any quadrilateral have an interesting property. Construct them, and figure out what property they have.

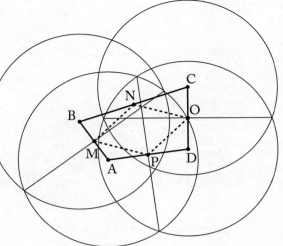

1. In the space below, locate any four noncollinear points A, B, C, and D.

2. Connect the points to form quadrilateral ABCD, as shown in the picture.

3. Choose any radius longer than half the longest side. Draw two circles, with centers A and B.

4. Connect the intersection points of circles A and B to find the midpoint, M.

5. Keeping the same radius, draw the circle with center C. Connect the intersection points of circles B and C to find the midpoint, N.

6. Keeping the same radius, draw the circle with center D. Connect the intersection points of circles C and D to find the midpoint, O.

7. Connect the intersection points of circles D and A to find the midpoint, P.

8. Connect the midpoints to form quadrilateral MNOP.

a.  What special type of quadrilateral is MNOP? _____

To verify this conjecture, draw $\overline{AC}$ and answer these questions:

b.  Which segment is the midsegment of $\triangle ABC$ ? _____

c.  Which segment is the midsegment of $\triangle ADC$ ? _____

d.  Why is $\overline{MN}$ parallel to $\overline{OP}$?

_____

_____

e.  Why are $\overline{MN}$ and $\overline{OP}$ the same length?

_____

_____

f.  Why is MNOP the special type of quadrilateral you declared it to be?

_____

_____

Name_____ Date_____

# Lesson 7.3
## Join the Midpoints of a Rectangle and Peer Into the Infinitesimal

1. Open your compass radius to the length of $\overline{AB}$. Construct circles with centers A, B, C, and D.

2. Connect appropriate intersections of these circles to locate the midpoints of rectangle ABCD. Label them E, F, G, and H. (These are shown in the example figure to the right.)

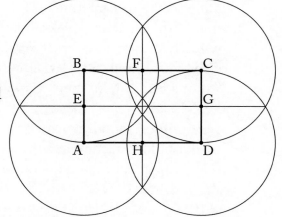

3. Connect these midpoints to form quadrilateral EFGH.

4. Draw diagonals $\overline{BD}$ and $\overline{AC}$.

5. Diagonals $\overline{BD}$ and $\overline{AC}$ intersect the sides of EFGH in midpoints I, J, K, and L. Label these midpoints. Connect them to form quadrilateral IJKL.

6. Diagonals $\overline{EG}$ and $\overline{FH}$ intersect the sides of IJKL in their midpoints; connect these midpoints to form another quadrilateral.

7. Continue connecting midpoints to get smaller and smaller quadrilaterals. In theory, you could go on forever.

a. What special type of quadrilateral is EFGH? _____

b. What special type of quadrilateral is IJKL? _____

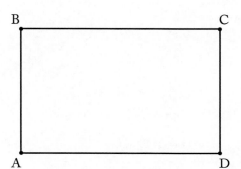

# Lesson 7.4
# Fill a Golden Rectangle to the Infinitesimal

Some rectangles are long and thin, and others are square. Since the time of the ancient Greeks, many people have felt that the most perfectly proportioned rectangle is the golden rectangle. The pillars of the Parthenon, the Cathedral of Notre Dame, and the United Nations Building in New York all utilize the golden rectangle in their design.

A **golden rectangle** can be divided into a square and another, smaller golden rectangle.

1. Open your compass radius to length GO. Swing an arc with center G from O across $\overline{GD}$. Label the point where the arc crosses $\overline{GD}$, E.

2. Keeping the same radius, draw an arc with center O across $\overline{OL}$. Label the intersection point, N.

3. Connect $\overline{EN}$ to form square GONE and another golden rectangle, LDEN.

4. Repeat this procedure to divide each golden rectangle into a square and a smaller golden rectangle, as far as you can. In theory, you could go on forever.

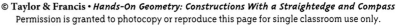

Name_____     Date_____

# Lesson 7.5
# Calculate the Golden Ratio

(For students who can use the quadratic formula.)

Many of the rectangles we use every day are close to being golden. File cards are 3 × 5, 4 × 6, or 5 × 8, and legal-size paper is 8½ × 14; these shapes are very close to being golden rectangles. Leonardo da Vinci showed that many of the proportions of the human body and face are based on the golden rectangle, and he used golden rectangles to place key features in his painting, *Mona Lisa*.

How do you determine the shape of the golden rectangle? The shape of any rectangle is determined by the ratio of its length to its width. For a square, this ratio is 1. For other rectangles, this ratio could be any number from 1 to infinity.

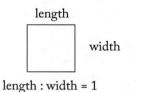

length : width = 1

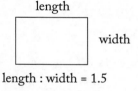

length : width = 1.5

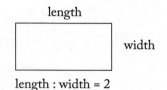

length : width = 2

The ratio of length to width of a golden rectangle is called the **golden ratio**.

a.  Compare the golden rectangle to the right to the rectangles shown above. What number would you guess to be close to the golden ratio?

_____

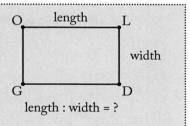

length : width = ?

To calculate the golden ratio exactly, consider golden rectangle GOLD, which has length GD = $x$ and width LD = 1. Hence $\frac{x}{1}$ must be the golden ratio. We can divide GOLD into the 1 × 1 square GONE and the smaller golden rectangle LDEN, which has length 1 and width $x - 1$. Hence $\frac{1}{x-1}$ must also be the golden ratio. Thus we get the equation $\frac{x}{1} = \frac{1}{x-1}$.

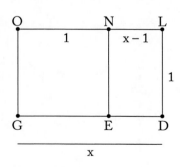

b.  Show how to use the quadratic formula to solve the above equation and find the exact form for the golden ratio (which is often called $f$, *phi*).

# Lesson 7.6
## Construct a Golden Rectangle

As you calculated in Lesson 7.5, the golden ratio is $\phi = \frac{1+\sqrt{5}}{2}$.
Note that this expression takes the square root of the integer 5, adds 1, and then divides by 2. All of these operations can be shown to be **constructible**. (We will investigate construction arithmetic in Chapter 10.) Given segment $\overline{GO}$ below that has length 1, it is possible to construct a perpendicular segment $\overline{OL}$ that has length $\phi = \frac{1+\sqrt{5}}{2}$.

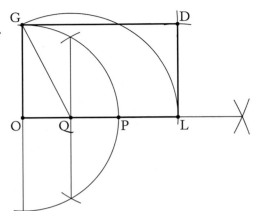

1. Extend ray $\overrightarrow{GO}$.

2. Erect a perpendicular to $\overline{GO}$ through O.

3. Locate point P on that perpendicular such that OP = OG.

4. Find the midpoint of $\overline{OP}$; label it Q. Draw $\overline{GQ}$.

5. Draw an arc with center Q and radius QG; label the point where the arc crosses the ray $\overrightarrow{OP}$, L. Point L is the third corner of the golden rectangle.

6. Draw an arc with radius OG and center L; draw an arc with radius OL and center G; label the intersection of these arcs D. D is the fourth corner of the rectangle.

7. Connect golden rectangle GOLD.

Why does this construction work? Because $GO = 1$, $OQ = \frac{1}{2}$, and, by the Pythagorean Theorem, $GQ = \frac{\sqrt{5}}{2}$; therefore, $OL = \frac{1+\sqrt{5}}{2}$.

G.

O.

Name_____     Date_____

# Lesson 7.7
# Construct a Regular Pentagon

As you have worked through these lessons, you have constructed an equilateral triangle, a square, and a regular hexagon, octagon, and dodecagon. But you have not yet constructed a **regular pentagon** that has five equal sides and five equal angles. The construction is tricky, but fun. Be precise and use a sharp pencil!

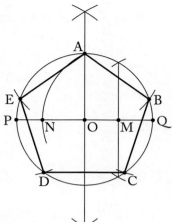

1.  Construct the perpendicular bisector of $\overline{PQ}$ below. Label the midpoint O.

2.  Draw the circle with center O and passing through P and Q.

3.  Label the point where the circle crosses the perpendicular above O, A.

4.  Construct the midpoint of $\overline{OQ}$; label it M. (Hint: Don't change the radius; draw arcs with center Q.)

5.  Draw an arc with center M and radius MA. Label the point where the arc crosses $\overline{PQ}$, N.

6.  Open your compass radius to the length AN. This is a side of your pentagon. Draw two arcs with center A that cross circle O. Label the left intersection E and the right one B.

7.  Keeping the same radius, draw an arc with center B across the circle; label the intersection point C. Draw another arc with center E across the circle; label the intersection point D.

8.  Draw the five sides of the regular pentagon ABCDE.

P._____.Q

# Answers

**Lesson 1.3**

B is the center.

**Lesson 2.2**

The diagonals of a nonconvex kite do not
  intersect.

**Lesson 2.3**

  a. Right
  b. Equal
  c. Equal
  d. Equal

**Lesson 3.5**

Two

**Lesson 3.6**

  a. Two
  b. The nine points are: three midpoints,
    three altitudes' feet, and three points
    midway from a foot to the orthocenter.

**Lesson 4.3**

Opposite sides of a rectangle are parallel and
  equal in length.

**Lesson 4.4**

The diagonals of a rectangle are equal, and
  they bisect each other.

**Lesson 4.5**

  a. A possible method:
    2. Open the compass to radius DC.
    3. Draw an arc with center D; label the
      point where the arc crosses *m*, A.
    4. Draw an arc with center A to the right
      of A.
    5. Draw an arc with center C above C.
    6. Label the point where the arcs cross, B.
    7. Draw ABCD.
  b. A square's diagonals are equal in length,
    are perpendicular to each other, bisect
    each other, and bisect the angles of the
    square.

**Lesson 5.4**

  a. Yes
  b. Yes
  c. Yes
  d. Yes
  e. Yes
  f. ii
  g. No
  h. No
  i. No
  j. Yes

**Lesson 5.6**

  1. Draw arc with radius PS and center R.
  2. Draw arc with radius SR and center P.
  3. Label the point where the two arcs cross,
    Q.
  4. Draw PQRS.

**Lesson 6.1**

  a. Flip it over side 3.
  b. Yes, because one will fit on top of the
    other.
  c. Yes, because the two triangles you can
    construct are identical.
  d. Yes
  e. Side 3 is too long, so side 1 and side 2
    can't reach each other.
  f. It must be that side $3 <$ side $1 +$ side $2$
  g. Yes

**Lesson 6.2**

  a. Kite
  b. Three
  c. Parallelogram
  d. Three
  e. The midsegment is half as long as the side
    it is parallel to.
  f. The grey triangle has one quarter the area
    of the white triangle.
  g. An isosceles trapezoid is formed.

**Lesson 6.4**

  a. The rays don't intersect.

b. No

c. 180°. Because the sum of all three angles of a triangle is 180°, the sum of any two angles must be less than 180°.

d. Yes

## Lesson 6.5

a. Yes

b. Yes

c. No, the construction method will work for any side lengths.

d. Yes, as long as the angle is between 0° and 180°.

## Lesson 6.6

a. Yes

b. Yes

c. Make side 2 longer than side 1.

d. SsA determines a triangle whenever the side opposite the angle is bigger than the side adjacent to the angle; in SsA, the S opposite the A is bigger than the s next to the A.

e. Yes

f. No

g. No

h. Yes

i. Yes

j. Yes

k. Two

l. No

m. Yes

n. Angle C is a right angle.

o. Yes

p. No

q. No

r. SSA determines a triangle when . . .

i. opposite > adjacent and the angle is obtuse, right, or acute.

ii. opposite = adjacent and the angle is acute.

iii. opposite < adjacent, the angle is acute.

iv. The triangle formed is a right triangle.

## Lesson 7.1

They are parallel and the midsegment is half as long as the base.

## Lesson 7.2

a. MNOP is a parallelogram.

b. $\overline{MN}$

c. $\overline{OP}$

d. As midsegments, both $\overline{MN}$ and $\overline{OP}$ are parallel to $\overline{AC}$, so they are parallel to each other.

e. Both $\overline{MN}$ and $\overline{OP}$ are half as long as $\overline{AC}$, so they are the same length.

f. Because MNOP has two opposite sides that are parallel and equal, MNOP must be a parallelogram.

## Lesson 7.3

a. a rhombus

b. a rectangle

## Lesson 7.5

a. Answers will vary; about 1.6.

b. $\phi = \frac{1+\sqrt{5}}{2}$

# Common Core State Standards Alignment

| Grade Level | Common Core State Standards in Math |
|---|---|
| Grade 4 | 4.MD.C Geometric measurement: understand concepts of angle and measure angles. |
| | 4.G.A Draw and identify lines and angles, and classify shapes by properties of their lines and angles. |
| Grade 5 | 5.G.B Classify two-dimensional figures into categories based on their properties. |
| Grade 7 | 7.G.A Draw construct, and describe geometrical figures and describe the relationships between them. |
| Grade 8 | 8.G.A Understand congruence and similarity using physical models, transparencies, or geometry software. |
| High School | HSG-CO.A Experiment with transformations in the plane. |
| | HSG-CO.B Understand congruence in terms of rigid motions. |
| | HSG-CO.C Prove geometric theorems. |
| | HSG-CO.D Make geometric constructions. |

**Key:** MD = Measurement & Data; G = Geometry; HSG-CO = High School Geometry – Congruence

*9 781593 634186*

BW - #0001 - 260723 - C0 - 276/219/5 - PB - 9781593634186 - Gloss Lamination